A Man Who Lives in a Dream

a poem

A Man Who Lives in a Dream

a poem

Garrett Buhl Robinson

Poet in the Park

In Humanity I see Grace, Beauty and Dignity.

Poet in the Park.com

A computer can count forever
but only a human mind can envision infinity.

— Denis Guedj

A Man
Who Lives
in a
Dream

a poem

Garrett
Buhl
Robinson

Proem

I have been told I have a sleep disorder
    but the prognosis may be relative.
I can manage to keep my life in order
    without disruptions to the way I live.

As an architect I design what's built,
    providing places where we live and work.
The finished buildings are concrete and real
    but they were only misty dreams at first.

Everyone tends to wander off in thought
    in their contemplation and speculation
and the plots of our developing lots
    are figments of the imagination.

With this in mind I hope you'll be amused
    with my lyrical lines of didactics
but to begin I must confess to you
    I am a narcoleptic architect.

1.

Some take a nap, but I find this funny,
    because my naps always seem to take me.
Often I cannot discern or perceive
    if I am in or outside of my dreams.

Some people will say that they go to sleep
    but everywhere I go, sleep goes with me.
For me to sleep and wake are not distinct.
    Maybe to me life's one continuous dream.

We segment seas from one body of water,
    and the divisions may be our own fiction
and the distinctions within the mind's matter
    are like swaying tides at different continents.

How do we really know the world we see?
    Isn't perception imaginary?
It's all a matter of neurology,
    so then, isn't thinking really a dream?

Descartes would wake up but then stay in bed
    and after sleep he would meditate,
but wondering inside his capacious head
    was he only dreaming he was awake?

One morning before he rose for his day
    he filled the space of his place with his graphs,
conceiving his Cartesian coordinates
    to provide us a new way to see math.

Did he exist to think or think he exists?
    Did he dream he woke or believe he slept?
Or is there really any difference
    since all that he knew happened in his head?

Are thoughts relatable things we can share
    or are they uniquely individual?
Can discrete beings be perfectly paired?
    What is popular about the personal?

If someone hears about what I have dreamed
    are they able to dream my dream with me
or would it be another way to see
    their own personal reality?

How do we discern what really exists?
    Do thoughts exist if they are not explained?
Do things exist that we do not witness?
    Don't rocks have mass whether or not they're weighed?

A face has features even in the dark
    but does beauty exist without a witness?
Quality could never fulfill its mark
    with no way to ponder and confirm it.

And quantity is of little difference
    with no consideration of amount,
there would not be a means of measurement
    without any ability to count.

And when considering just how we count
    is it a reality or a dream?
How can we begin numbering amounts
    when there is only one of everything?

Certainly there are similarities,
    and what is shared makes everything complete
but every single individual thing
    is in itself entirely unique.

The fact that we dream, no one will deny,
    so unquestionably our dreams exist
and what can be imagined in our minds
    can be developed to a larger context.

If I'm awake or if I am asleep
    either way I'm the same human being
and if I can dream a reality,
    there must be reality to my dream.

And what we can conceive within the mind
    is absolutely endless in potential
to be freely shaped and changed in design
    from the particular to the universal.

And even if we have no certainty
    precisely where all of the things may fit,
we have a sense for the absurdity
    as we all know that all we know is limited.

Everything changes yet remains complete
    and every action will have a response.
It's a strict system of causality
    breaking just as it is making the bonds.

Certainly some will deny this decree
    but I would love to hear how they respond.
Do they believe the universe a machine
    that's plugged into some socket from beyond?

Thinking people are just what the world needs
    to do more in life than just eat and breed
and bring more dreams into reality
    with neurological activity.

2.

To me it can be the funniest thing
    that the very moment I drift to sleep
I immediately begin to dream
    and I don't know where the distinctions meet.

It is like walking through an open door,
    traversing from one chamber to the next,
elevators going from floor to floor
    or an escalator's revolving steps.

Each passage is a variated phase
    as well as a distinctive destination.
I move through time whether I go or stay,
    and my body is my lifelong location.

And even when I move from state to state
    I will continue to reside in me
and whether I am dreaming or awake
    it's a continuous reality.

Some people work for their entire lives,
    some work for their responsibilities.
I'm always residing within my mind
    and I persist in working through my dreams.

But this isn't particular to me,
    it's just the perfect fit for what I do.
No matter who you are, you have to sleep,
    and when you dream, you're making new worlds too.

From one to all we're making up our minds
    in the degrees of sensibility.
It is our life, we do it all the time,
    our creativity comes naturally.

If you have any doubts about this thought,
    keep in mind when you read you're thinking this
and whether you contemplate it or not
    in our thinking is where these thoughts exists.

There's some who say the dream is in our head.
    Others insist our head is in a dream.
How do we comprehend something that's said?
    How do we understand what it may mean?

There's more than the identity of words
    or the components placed inside a phrase.
It is the melody as it is heard
    in the situation where it is played.

There's no distinction from one to another
    in the continuity of the whole.
At that point what we all know is a wonder
    and then we wonder what all we may know.

I told my boss that I'm narcoleptic
    and she still insisted on hiring me.
The only way I know how to address this
    is she just gave me the job of my dreams.

She was direct and did not hesitate,
    "I expect you to create, not conform.
I'm not concerned about your mental state
    but how you professionally perform."

Now I am working in a room with others
    with our assignments and specific tasks
and none of my coworkers seem to bother
    if I am ever slumped over my desk.

In fact my coworkers are all amazed,
    but there are also times when they are stunned,
that I can sleep through the whole business day
    yet I am able to get my work done.

They say it is something that is unheard,
    that I am soundly sleeping with closed eyes
yet somehow my hand continues to work
    and I dream up incredible designs.

I say, "I don't mean to be obnoxious.
    I work outside conventions and confines
and when I tip into the unconscious
    I whirl in currents of the fluid mind."

It's an oddity and anomaly
    but I've developed a proficiency.
I can do this work while I'm fast asleep
    and I do it best while I'm in my dreams.

My boss says she's thrilled with my performance.
    She doesn't fret or cause a commotion.
She lets me grind away while in my trance
    and only wakes me for a promotion.

3.

When I find myself drifting off to sleep
    a part of wakefulness remains with me.
I bring the world with me into my dream
    — an imaginary reality.

Sometimes I wonder if we dream designs
    or do the designs organize our lives?
Do we live in constructions of the mind
    where form and function carefully align?

Do I draw what I dream or dream I draw
    or does it have to be the way it seems?
Can I believe all that I thought I saw
    or does belief determine what I see?

We may expect some particular function
    that serves a specific utility.
A closure of a corridor means nothing
    if it doesn't have a single opening.

So we always need some sort of entrance
    providing access inside of the space
and these considerations will enhance
    how the shape designates what may take place.

And then there are always more than people
    who will need to get inside the space too.
There has to be some way to let in light.
    Windows are walls we're able to see through.

We need conduits for the circuit wiring
    and types of lines for communication.
Water is needed to pass through the plumbing
    for the refreshment of circulation.

I suppose it is curious to know
　　about all the designs that we create.
We are more concerned with what comes and goes
　　than the permanent fixtures of the place.

Of course possessions need to be secured
　　and set in place where they take up the space
but are they owned by where they are reserved
　　or take ownership of where they remain?

And in all the different corridors
　　who's expected to be the occupants?
Are they the workers or the customers?
　　Are they visiting guests or residents?

Is there a soft ambience of welcome
　　or stern assurance of security?
Should the arrangement give a subtle tone
　　or just make space for some utility?

Do they seek the sleek lines of glass and steel
　　or the rock hewn grandeur of a chateau?
Or how the warmth of grainy wood may feel
　　in cozy comforts of a snug abode?

Then by connecting all the corridors
　　with accessing passages leading through,
consider more than a long line of doors,
　　ponder where they're going and leading to.

The passages can provide refreshment
　　to stir the circulation through the place,
conducting the tempo of the movement
　　as they meander or tighten the pace.

There are proponents of utility
    and the promoters of efficiency
but there's more than getting from A to B,
    the best discoveries are found in between.

And transits are their own experience
    in the departure and destination,
as an elevation at an entrance
    can be an uplifting inspiration.

Trees in the courtyard can revitalize
    with a whisper of soft breeze where the shade is
and arrangements of plants in a design
    can turn a break room into an oasis.

And how are rooms and passages attached?
    Are they like berries lined along a stem?
Or are the rooms like seeds waiting to hatch
    with the warm layers enfolding them in?

Do the arrangements draw people together
    so they pour into an expanding sea?
Do they create a breadth and depth of water
    for the currencies of economy?

Or are the workstations more like springboards
    projecting attention into the open,
launching boldly into future endeavors
    like the dandelion's seeds softly floating?

Are they intended to be modular,
    adjusting arrangements for diverse projects,
balancing specific with versatile
    in powerful interactive dynamics?

Then the entire space can be rearranged
    to effectively address each assignment.
The same space can be made in different shapes
    with all the parts in intricate alignments.

For homes or businesses a building's structure
    is made for a certain facility
and what it is serving is always much more
    than just a reposeful residency.

Our houses and buildings accommodate
    flourishing organizations of life,
families and businesses aggregate
    to assemble into ascending heights.

4.

When I'm asleep and also while awake,
    especially when I do not know which,
my thoughts continue pouring on the page
    outlining ideas my drawings depict.

I start with two dimensions from the lot,
    the space of ground where we intend to build,
then from this footprint I can start to plot
    and develop through the vertical field.

There are allowances of open space
    and the providence to facilitate
and places where we can accommodate
    depend on the arrangements we create.

But just as much as the structure's design,
    the various equations' calculations
must balance factors such as place and time,
    the neighborhood and the orientation.

Building a building in a city grid
    is more than developing a construction,
a promenading place is being made
    within a historical conversation.

There are the casual and the formal
    but they all have to carry their own weight.
If they make an entrance in this grand ball,
    they must have something credible to say.

Of course function is the necessity
    to perform at whatever task they do,
but mingling together for centuries
    the elegance of form's important too.

Some are standing stolid with chiseled stone,
　　some tower to be seen all over town,
some touch upon the most delicate tone
　　and prance in an enchanting crystal gown.

They dance in traffic spinning at their feet,
　　the swirling surges of society.
The commerce is their music's melody
　　that thrums inside with their occupancy.

Discussing matters of our tradition,
　　they speak the language of humanity.
It is an ongoing conversation
　　of accommodated activity.

But admittedly they don't have to speak
　　and may still participate in the dance,
sometimes the grandest way they can proceed
　　is in the quiet grace by which they stand.

Although they may appear to be transfixed
　　along the streets in stationary lines,
they can be considered intrepid ships
　　that sail across expansive seas of time.

The craft and care with which they're put together
　　is more than just comportment and composure.
Since they are offering others their shelter
　　they must live in perpetual exposure.

Each day with people on and off the street
　　they draw and send with contacts near and far.
Then rise through night in soft and lofty sleep
　　to sparkle in the sky with quiet stars.

5.

While I'm working on one of my designs
    it's like the bouncing of a rubber ball.
I am not nodding off into my sleep,
    I'm arcing deeper into what I draw.

All I am melts into a swirling liquid
    I pour into the process of my work.
It is the fluent labor of a mystic,
    a flow that fills the passages and turns.

My practice is also my directive
    that I adjust to any application.
It is my life and my life's objective,
    sustaining by providing destinations.

Like breath I alternate from slump to swell,
    the wave of an uninterrupted line,
a floating plume lifted from an ink well
    as I continue pouring out designs.

The lines I draw do more than just partition,
    they're strings on music's dulcet instruments,
a play within the space of an invention,
    the keys of themes to different denizens.

The compass is one of my guiding gauges
    to measure different scales accurately,
ensuring that the sketches on the pages
    will correspond with physicality.

The compass rounds out an elegant arc
    while standing for a pivot's sweeping turn
and Newton would love this wandering star
    to calculate the area under this curve.

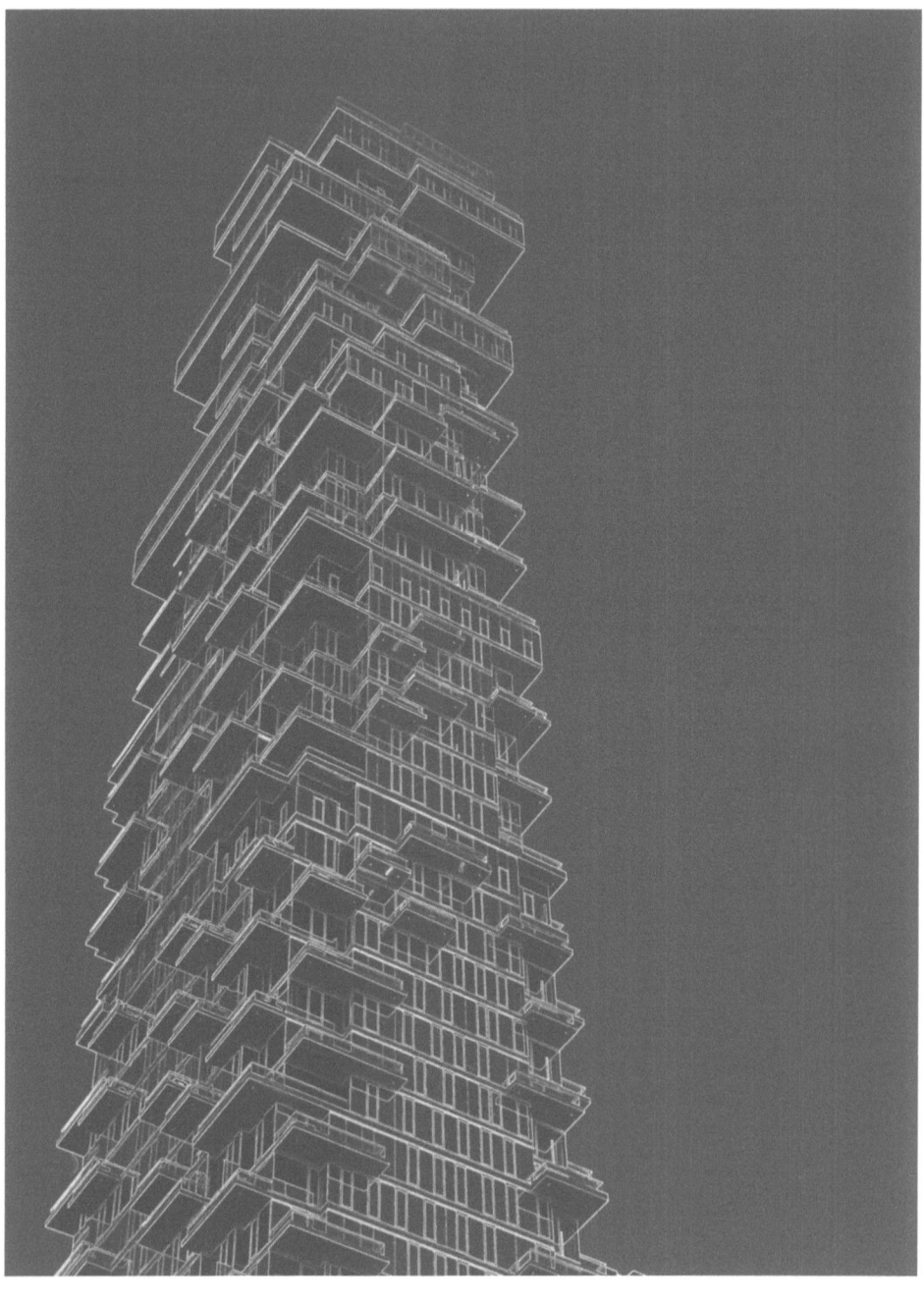

I make computations with integration
    but I measure space in a different way,
I concentrate on the facilitation
    and the activities that fill the space.

And with the compass' curve or a straight edge,
    I'm endlessly intrigued with drawing lines.
They angle up and also plumb the depths
    while sketching an eternity of time.

A line can trace the shape of everything,
    the paragon of pure simplicity,
continuous in singularity
    yet incremented to infinity.

The line defines as well as it creates.
    It can unravel as well as bind.
It measures the expanse of endless space
    and lightly arcs at the height of the sky.

Lines can meet at the point of an angle
    and also wave seductively as lace.
Lines can run platonic in parallel
    yet still touch on the curvatures of space.

They figure features for a silhouette,
    follow the swaying fall of a soft feather
or take the distance that is the shortest
    or they can simply continue forever.

6.

And yet what is my greatest interest
    is not the lines I draw in my designs,
my whole intention is the allowance
    for the lines in the course of people's lives.

The lines of people's lives aren't on the drafts
    and yet their presence is always implied.
They're present in the spaces where they pass
    and open corridors where they unwind.

There are considerations of logistics
    for currents through which people come and go.
It is no different than fluid dynamics
    in managing an unrestricted flow.

The complications are the intersections
    where streams and currents meet and overlap.
They can also flow in distinct directions
    while together in the same channeled path.

A river is composed of particles
    with a single mind for gravity,
but the people can be a debacle —
    each with its own intentionality.

There are some who will wander and meander,
    while others want to rush directly through.
Some flock together like geese in a gander,
    others muse through the window's open view.

The passages are made with one intent —
    to get the people to their destinations.
The objective here is in the movement
    where relocation is the occupation.

Then the variety of corridors
    arranged along the halls where they refer,
gathering and releasing through the doors
    while inside they spool and unspool in turn.

Some chambers are an eddy's whirling pool
    where lines of currents swirl in soft repose
while frothing with refreshments stirring cool
    so intense competition can mellow.

Others may twist and loop to tie in knots
    so the different lines may together hold,
some hitched, some square, secure and holding taut,
    some looped and laced into elegant bows.

Others splice and twine into sturdy cables
    for loads from industrial factories.
Others stretch across looms and spin from tables
    for knits of cloth and weaves of tapestries.

But the singular lines that make me wonder
    are the lines working in solitary.
They don't stitch and tie together with others
    instead they reel into the mystery.

Of course there can't be complete isolation,
    we all need some type of social exchange,
and life depletes in vacant dissipation
    without anything to pursue or gain.

Yet, when someone has time to be alone
    and ponder beyond convention's expectance
and devote one's attention on one's own
    directing development through one's interest

then in the vast space and time spent alone
 even if someone seems consumed with oneself,
one may devote oneself through the unknown
 and then offer more for everyone else.

For one to accomplish something in life
 of which all our needs and desires insist,
there is the obvious demand for time
 otherwise movement could never exist.

Everyone knows our spatial dimensions
 most commonly called breadth and length and depth...
and of course there is the fourth addition
 along time discrete or continuous.

But I am not restricted to these limits,
 nor do they confine anybody else.
We all live in infinite dimensions
 whether or not anyone else can tell.

Before you say I'm a deluded fool
 take a few things into consideration —
to accomplish anything we need a tool
 and our greatest tool is the imagination.

The best tool can shape and orientate
 for the demands of any application
then may adjust to what one designates
 so it can work for the desired intention.

Our imaginations may conceive
 the aim and purpose for each task at hand,
then expand beyond all we ever see
 to encompass all we can understand.

Some said in the past we weren't meant to fly
    but following some logic step by step,
one can find oneself perched up in the sky
    on a high rises' observation deck.

The different dimensions are levels
    we must maintain for our activities
and what we sustain with these different levels
    is the allowance of our faculties.

When everyone's young they need space to grow
    and this space comes in a number of fields.
There are families, games, the thrills and woes
    but our intelligence is just as real.

Even though the space where our minds extend
    may be considered detached and abstract,
that doesn't mean that it doesn't exist,
    we know their reality for a fact.

When I open and read into a book
    a passage is extending before me.
It is an alternate world where I look
    into the expanse of mentality.

Some may say we cannot travel through time
    yet we do when we study history,
reading the minds in what others describe
    to bridge the past and contemporary.

Some see no point in learning about math
    yet we are constantly calculating.
We give and take as we add and subtract
    to find solutions for difficulties.

Some may say that there are more direct ways
    to interact besides reading and writing,
and do we really mean all that we say
    through all the fluff and frills of poetry?

Why not streamline all our interaction
    on the principles of efficiency?
Yet unnecessary explorations
    are what lead us to our discoveries.

Considering this, one has to admit
    there are countless dimensions of allowance
to pursue intent for accomplishment
    and engage any distinguishing talent.

This isn't some detached escapism,
    it's not fantasy or a silly show,
the mind is certainly real, it exists
    and in a way, it is all that we know.

Society is a place to explore
    and we pursue life through our engagements,
but considering all the walls and doors,
    they were all first drawn on a drafting table.

It is the great paradox of our being
    in the perplexities of reality,
the mind is our sole means for understanding
    yet it remains an endless mystery.

7.

I made a choice others would not expect
    and some say my reasoning was too guarded.
They thought it odd I'd be an architect
    when I come from a family of artists.

But it has never ceased to surprise me
    when I hear people express their confusion.
There is a need for creativity
    in every direction of our professions.

The act of creation is an arrangement
    with sequences of new associations.
No one can live in total isolation.
    We are generated in combinations.

Or course, this is done between two people
    but it can also be done on one's own
when a person seeks out one's own interest
    to find where they feel comfortably at home.

So in this regard one can find a space
    to pursue what appeals to one's own tastes
and in this personal and private place
    one can arrange one's interest and create.

What's the difference between an architect
    and what you believe to be an artist?
Aren't we all looking for ways to direct
    and receive one another's interests?

Is not every artistic expression
    a residence for the imagination?
It is a statement of arranged impressions
    intended to allure investigation.

One may paint vivid images on canvas
    where talent and inspiration combine,
an expression's amusing dalliance
    rendered through skills painstakingly refined.

The painters certainly have their intentions,
    perhaps something specific to portray,
but the reaction of the audience
    is something no one can anticipate.

And during the creation of the work
    the artist's focus resides in the frame
and within the completion of the work
    part of the artist always will remain.

Then through the audience's musing gaze
    they may be excited with the expression
but after the audience walks away
    the art resides in them as an impression.

Whether our profession or residence,
    both pursuits are the same in many ways.
We do not live where we are set or rest.
    We truly live where we are most engaged.

At work I may delineate a space
    and for the design receive a credit
but we all know what really makes the place
    is all of the life that occupies it.

So artistic expression is a place,
    technique and media are the setting,
where artist and audience may exchange
    each other's interest and inspiration.

There are the gifts of the artist's creation
    and gifts in the audience's attention
but in a way they start looking the same
    since gifts must be received as much as given.

Some artists say their work is the audience
    by opening minds through their expressions
and the public's interest and attendance
    may goad and guide the artists' inventions.

And whether you are a devoted artist
    or a rapt member of the audience,
what is truly the finest work of art
    is the interactive experience.

The distinct and disjunctive components
    differing in their discrete form and substance
are all combined with the artistic talents
    to offend or append a sort or sense.

A person can work at the job's location
    to support a family that stays at home,
as artists refine their communication
    in isolation and working alone.

And the different directions of our interests
    and the shared obligations of our time
provide the variety of elements
    with which we make our individual lives.

And in my architectural arrangements
    and the fabrications of my designs
I am facilitating others interests
    to enable them to live their own lives.

There are needs to provide protective shelters
    preserving personal and private interests
and there are needs to release and unfetter
    through the necessity of openness.

My designs do not impose arrangements
    or enforce oppressive obligations.
They provide passages and corridors
    to allow open associations.

They are the variated calculations
    achieving and sustaining upright balance
that can facilitate our interaction
    through tight security and free allowance.

A composer creates an orchestration
    with arrangements of notes on the staffed page,
a singular organization
    that all the different musicians can play.

So I have not abandoned artistry
    for the base drudgery of application
and if some persist argumentatively
    there's something to take in consideration:

if art can be a solitary dream,
    it is a dream to be shared with the public
as society's a collective scheme
    to facilitate personal interest.

A carpenter builds a theater's stage
    that many may consider to be simple
but for sublime drama to be portrayed,
    the place for a performance is essential.

And even a residential apartment,
    the epitome of banality,
is a place for the most profound creation —
    the raising of a single family.

In reality we are all artists
    in what is both unexpected and planned,
each one of us takes our experience
    and makes it into what we understand.

8.

As I follow my regular routine
    and address demands each and every day,
drifting and waking through dream after dream,
    I wonder whose life I'm living anyway.

I would love to pursue my own interest
    aside from my responsibilities.
I have a life outside of this business
    and all the demands of society.

Is life an individual's self-drive
    or are we only what we hold together?
Do the buildings enable us to live
    or do we live for the buildings' endeavor?

We will pursue our lives' activities
    whether we're in or outside of the doors.
It's not the building that's determining
    what we each decide to live our lives for.

Then others may argue and make the claim
    that buildings enclose and confine us inside
but they also provide in other ways
    a place to nourish and preserve our lives.

Then through each one of our activities
    we are in turn enlivening the buildings,
and then the buildings we are animating
    become multi-personal organisms.

In the past we used furnaces and boilers
    and the buildings were types of animals.
Now cities begin to look more like forests
    with flourishing foliage of solar panels.

All the buildings provide us with our homes
    and our professional facilities.
They give us a place where we may belong
    while they ease our lives with amenities.

And in practically any residency
    where people live and make their private homes,
they can enjoy domestic luxuries
    that in the past kings and queens did not own.

As they empower us to achieve success
    and we are soothed with luxuries they lend,
this may all be in their own interest,
    they may do this so we'll make more of them.

If buildings are hives consider the bees,
    and this may allow us to understand,
bees don't make as much honey as they need,
    the bees make as much honey as they can.

Then the more they produce, the more they grow
    and we see nature's invisible hand,
they don't proliferate by what they know,
    they simply follow supply and demand.

Yet if they grow past what they can sustain
    they're earlier success becomes a trap
and the unsustainable population
    will lead to a catastrophic collapse.

As I'm committed to our liberty
    my architecture makes a declaration —
to sustain freedom indefinitely
    we must exercise self-regulation.

A rush to lead is not a victory.
 It's too easy to lose what's gained in haste.
The greatest and truest victory
 is the victory that we can sustain.

There may be a building I can design
 that soars to the height of infinity
and even if I see it in my mind
 it may only be a hyperbole.

I can think of something impractical
 like skyscrapers that are made out of wood
but just because I think it can be built
 doesn't necessarily mean it should.

A city's not developed and sustained
 with any singular organization.
It's interlocking links of a long chain
 through successions of many generations.

Every building is a legacy
 and to ensure that they are all protected,
there is a protocol of policy
 safeguarding them against the unexpected.

Some may consider this to be oppressive,
 that growth is stifled with stiff regulation,
but they provide additional protection
 while fostering ingenious innovation.

I am for a fluid society
 but there is also practicality,
if society flows completely free
 then there wouldn't be any standing buildings.

Our need for water is a good example
        and refreshment is something we all need
but we would all be sipping out of puddles
        without a solid cup to hold a drink.

Enforcing the standards of building codes
        ensures we can all keep working together
to build private buildings on common roads
        without toppling over each other.

This is quite simple yet it's complicated
        but I think every person will agree,
in our own ways, we all desire the same,
        ultimately, we all want to succeed.

So by checking our special interests
        we may maximize our collective gains.
We will always be greater together
        when we agree on this singular aim.

9.

Every day at the office while we work
    and I am drifting in and out of sleep,
my coworkers do not become perturbed,
    I'm an intriguing curiosity.

It seldom causes any complications
    but sometimes there can be a little strain,
when there is a lapse of communication
    because we are living on different planes.

It's not a hierarchy low or high
    comparing levels of our consciousness,
but it is not always easy to find
    where all the paths connect and intersect.

And I need to be more considerate
    because it must look a little eerie
as they watch me drafting elaborate
    designs while I am obviously sleeping.

But beyond the peculiar observations
    there are a number of crucial instants
necessitating our communication
    to coordinate all of our assignments.

One may have a very specific task
    yet we must work together as a team
and I can't always work straight through my naps
    on soaring towers in my misty dreams.

I can hear subtle voices down a hall,
    a distinct yet a distant summoning,
"Oscar, Oscar" as my coworkers call
    then touch my arm as they gently wake me.

It can be startling to be awoken,
    an abrupt alteration of a phase.
It is like something is suddenly broken
    before a complete cycle can be made.

We all have rhythms that are all our own
    and sometimes we must stop and calibrate,
yet when I move and snooze within my zone
    it's jolting when someone slams on the brakes.

It's like I hear them speaking from outside
    a building where I'm sketching a design,
a celestial voice I don't recognize
    out beyond where my attention resides.

I will open my eyes into the place
    I don't immediately recognize.
I may stare up into a stranger's face
    to see perplexity in squinting eyes.

I'll push myself back from the drafting table
    and then turn my head in a sweeping gaze
trying to identify my location
    while I am peering through a foggy haze.

We all have a tendency to be self-consumed
    and our demands of life will often clash.
We may blur everything else in a room
    to focus on a single, narrow task.

Perhaps I am inclined to be dramatic
    and feel compelled to leap to the extremes.
I can tend to detach from interaction
    as I am isolated in my dreams.

But in the stages of my awakening,
    the fuzz will sharpen into clarity
as I keep hearing other people saying,
    "Oscar!" then I remember — Oh, that's me.

Then we discus until we reach agreement
    and I admit the confusion was mine.
Then we coordinate all our assignments
    so we can stay together in step and time.

10.

Through my experience and interaction
    I have realized that the way people speak
and various ways of communication
    are different phenomena to me.

I know when some are having conversations
    they have very specific things to say
and as I know they are communicating
    my senses seem to work in a weird way.

All of the words they use are signifiers
    arranged by rules of the syntactic line.
It is a sequence of identities
    acting out events in a person's mind.

It is fascinating when they create
    another reality that's not there.
It is a universe made of language
    as they draw a new world out of thin air.

To me, sound is almost like a texture.
    While I am working at my drafting table
what I see are ripples of air pressure,
    sonic waves that bubble and bounce in space.

So when I am working on my designs
    there are scales to guide and edges to trace
but more than drawing the buildings and lines,
    I see activities that will take place.

Confinement and allowance must balance,
    there's ergonomic flow to calculate,
but the inspiration for my mind's palace
    is a dancer walking out on the stage.

The dancer needs the firmness of the floor
    to make her pivots, turns and roaring leaps
and even standing she appears to soar
    in the comportment of her artistry.

The floor is absolutely fundamental,
    the walls are the surrounding boundaries,
the ceiling shelters from the temperamental
    and the structure is a facility.

But what takes precedence in all I make
    is what the drawn enclosures can provide
and more than anything it is the space
    that will allow the life to live inside.

So when I'm sitting at my drafting table
    I start with an idea and a blank page
and from nothing begin to make arrangements
    like carving Petra from a rock's sheer face.

It's like the rigor of devoted dancers
    and all their sacrifices and commitment,
working their miracles inside their cloisters
    by drawing beauty out of emptiness.

And from the column of a stack of paper
    with practiced skill and notions of the mind,
I'll tediously sketch and draw and measure
    to make my imaginative designs.

There are variables to calculate
    that all work their way into the designs
but as much as the structure's load of weight,
    I must consider what the space provides.

Yet of the shapes of place I can create
    they can be little more than mere locations.
It is the occupants that elaborate
    all my professional delineations.

I can design all kinds of residence
    that any number of people could buy,
but what could ever be the sense to this
    if there was no one who could live inside.

I can make houses for people to use
    just as a bank can make a buyer's loan
but only the residents of a house
    can turn the place into a home.

Accounting for desirability
    from soft and quaint to rigid and concrete,
there are considerable qualities
    that real estate buyers will often seek.

There is what suits a certain neighborhood
    and feels to fit the best in that location.
They may want a safe place to raise their brood
    or make a daring avant-garde statement.

Yet beyond a conspicuous display,
    stern security or friendly welcome,
what we all want returning from our day
    is the comfort we feel when we come home.

So overlooking presentation's show,
    aside from fashion and desire for style
on cold and rainy nights what matters most
    is that we feel at ease and warm inside.

The threads of home are woven like a nest,
　　arrangements for our preferential tastes.
We surround ourselves with our interests
　　as we make the space our personal place.

As photographs are more than just the frames
　　for pictured portraits of a family.
They are the warm and sentimental passages
　　that lead to love and domesticity.

And little curios of relatives
　　that are carefully tucked where we can find
are keys that open our fond memories
　　— the safe and precious places in our minds.

And in the warmest folds of people's homes
　　I may be lucky enough to design,
are the events of love and happiness
　　that are carried and cherished throughout life.

Epilogue

We may find some lite humor in the question
    if explanations can be entertaining,
is there any hope this sort of expression
    could ever be amusing and engaging?

Some discourses are expository
    and are filled with methodical descriptions,
with textbook problems and abstract theory
    without artistic, poetic invention.

What often comes to mind with explanations
    are images of towering stacks of books,
but before we dismiss examinations
    we should first pause to take another look.

For example consider a dull stone,
    a pebble to serve as a gauge,
it may seem petty when it's all alone,
    yet without it, mountains could never be made.

There is a geologist whom I know well,
    you can show him any rock you can find,
and it provides a story he can tell
    that can illuminate eons of time.

So considering the act of instruction
    and the different ways we accomplish it,
I believe the greatest type of production
    is made in ways that we comprehend.

The validations that we find in life
    are the achievements that our time can span
and what satisfaction most fills our mind
    more than broadening what we understand?

Our bodies are relatively the same
    and being allows us a building's space,
when we exercise our capacious brains
    than the more rooms we have to entertain.

And when we consider entertainment
    and tuneful works of well composed amusement,
they are the ways of passionate engagement
    not the debauchery of rude confusion.

We cannot always frolic in the open
    because we'd be exposed when we need rest.
We balance the rigor of our devotion
    with the soft blessings of our happiness.

Whatever we enjoy we must preserve,
    what has value requires security,
and this is only provided through work
    or else it would be lost haphazardly.

So what joy is found in my little lines
    that I painstakingly tune with my music,
can be strummed with a reader's playful mind
    although they have the option to refuse it.

Perhaps it can be considered a game
    but please be practical with the fantastic,
to get the most enjoyment when you play
    you must develop with devoted practice.

Note

The phrase "Bees do not make as much honey as they need, they make as much honey as they can" on page 54, was heard by the poet at a beekeeping class in Brooklyn conducted by Chris Harp and Grai St. Clair Rice.

Acknowledgements

Many of the expressions in this poem have been inspired by the work of Eric Kandel. His ideas regarding the creativity inherit to sentience have impressed me profoundly. Of particular importance to this poem are the legendary public statements – C.P. Snow's lectures: *The Two Cultures* and G.H. Hardy's book: *A Mathematician's Apology*. I have also found endless amusement pondering the friendship of Richard Dawkins and Douglas Adams. I believe their friendship exemplifies the dynamic relationship between the sciences and the arts to provide an undeniable proof of their essential dependence upon one another. Also, I must recognize, Jean-Pierre Changeux, particularly from the book *Conversations on Mind, Matter and Mathematics* with Alain Connes, which I serendipitously discovered on the shelves of the Public Library in Portland, Oregon in the 1990's. This book, along with countless others, has guided and directed my development within some of the fields which this poem modestly refers. In addition to this, the life and work of the Bengali mathematician Srinivasa Ramanujan has been a source of inspiration. I would also like to thank members of my family, plus a number of friends and acquaintances for providing their patient attention and insightful comments as they listened to my rambling discourses upon some of these ideas. And for the enduring tradition of poetry – may the fluent music of language always provide humanity with refreshment, insight and inspiration so we never forget the limitless potential within us all.

Some other titles by Garrett Buhl Robinson

<u>Poetry</u>
Whispering Emily
The Ballad of Emperor Norton
Little Pieces of Poetry
City of Poems
The Nobody
Always Here Always Odd
Beauty beyond Reason
Martha, a poem

<u>Fiction</u>
Zoë
Nunatak

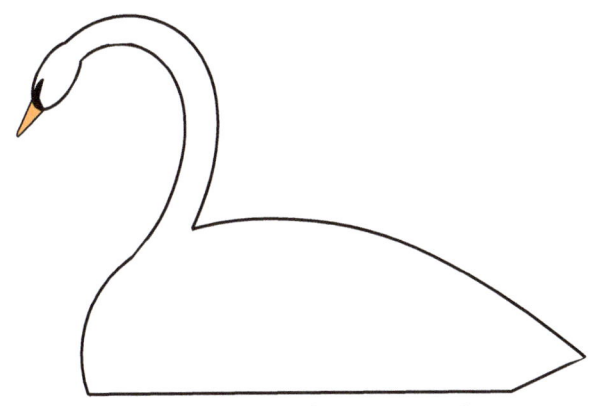

Poet in the Park
In Humanity I see Grace, Beauty and Dignity.

Poet in the Park.com

www.ingramcontent.com/pod-product-compliance
Lightning Source LLC
Chambersburg PA
CBHW040857120626
46551CB00001B/51